JAMIE MCKENDRICK
Ink Stone

faber and faber

First published in 2003
by Faber and Faber Limited
3 Queen Square London WC1N 3AU
Published in the United States by Faber and Faber Inc.,
an affiliate of Farrar, Straus and Giroux LLC, New York

Typeset by Faber and Faber Limited
Printed in England
by T J International Ltd, Padstow, Cornwall

A CIP record for this book
is available from the British Library

ISBN 0-571-21532-7

2 4 6 8 10 9 7 5 3 1

for Ba and Ed

Acknowledgements

I am grateful to the editors of the following newspapers, magazines and anthologies where some of these poems appeared: *Independent on Sunday, London Review of Books, Magma, Observer, Oxford Poetry, Poetry Review, Sciacallo, Stand, Times Literary Supplement*; and to the editors of the following anthologies: *'Earth has not anything to show more fair', Flora Poetica, Last Poems, New Writing 9, Poetry Seen: Portraits and Poems of Contemporary Liverpool Poets*; and to Wagner & Van Santen, who published a Dutch translation, *Een Versteende Dierentuin*, which included seven of these poems. I would also like to thank Tom Kuhn and Karen Leeder, editors of *Empedocles' Shoe: Essays on Brecht's Poetry*, for commissioning the Brecht poem and for their help with the German.

Contents

In China and Japan, the use of bottled ink is frowned upon and generally considered to be a concession to barbarians . . .

The older the stone that is used to make an ink stone, the better it will perform. Because the geological formations in China are much older than those in Japan, the best stones come from China . . . The Japanese term for the best grades of slate used in the manufacture of ink stones is *tankai*. There are several grades of *tankai* just as there are grades of diamonds. The very best *tankai* was found under rivers. Today it can only be found in private collections and museums. Since China has a long history, all the stones of this quality have already been found.

Steven L. Saitzyk, *Art Hardware*

So he vanish'd from my sight,
And I pluck'd a hollow reed,

And I made a rural pen,
And I stain'd the water clear

William Blake

Apotheosis

His bonce high-domed like a skep, the bee-man
holds forth on how to pick a bee up by its wings
which are strong enough – it stands to reason –
to bear the weight without harm to their hinges.
As though he were a banjo-player and the bee's wings
were a two-ply, fine abalone plectrum,
he demonstrates with a bumblebee on the windowframe
the exact grip between forefinger and thumb

but slips on the waxed oak floor, his arm outstretched,
neither tightening nor, regardless of his own fate,
loosening his hold on the bee one micro-notch.
I try to break his fall but move too late
for, with a dry hum, he streaks off out of reach
through the open window, still holding forth the bee.

Bee Lines

The novice keepers, togged in gloves and goggles,
smoked out the spirit of the hive and laid
three trays, each caked with hexagons,
on the oak table where they sat and ogled
the gold light trapped in the grid of cells
till their lids grew heavy and they trudged to bed.

Lying beside her husband, she wasn't sure
if she was the burglar or the burgled
caught napping as the whole place was stripped bare
but she dreamed herself on the crest of an elm
where a swarm was scouring half an eggshell
whilst the piping of the queen bestrode the air

dainty as a sea-chest in a maelstrom.
She woke to find a double stream
of bees, one coming down, the other climbing
the chimney, heaving bags of it back to the hive,
and when the last ingot had taken wing
the hearthstone was backlit like the gate of heaven.

Good Hedges

He wants the holly tree cut down to size,
the holly tree where the birds are sound, and safe
from his cat whose snickering impersonation
of birdsong – more like the din a mincer makes –
fools no one, and charms nothing out of the trees.

He wants us to tidy up the pyracantha sprouting
its fire-thorns and berry-laden fractals, and clip
the brambles, the lilacs, everything wild.
Next he'll want the hedgehog's spikes filed down,
the mole's claws bound up with green twine

– already he's replaced his own hair with ginger nylon.
His light he says is being blocked. It's dark
where he is. He has a point – so many deaths
in these few houses, it's like something
loosed from the Bible. One lucky escape, though:

the bearded roofer, one along, who lost
his footing, high on the scaffolding, and fell,
with his deck of tiles, on his shoulder and skull.
Sometimes tears come to his eyes for no reason
he can think of, but now the sun's out he sits again

on the patio, plucking from his banjo
some Appalachian strand of evergreen bluegrass,
then an Irish reel where his fingers scale
a glittering ladder like a waterfall
so even the songbirds hush in the holly tree.

For Now

I'm up in my watchtower, keeping watch over
the beasts of the field, now few enough,
the fowls of the air and the crooked ways of men,
through binoculars, when the doorbell rings
like a tinkling cymbal. Half-dressed,
I bound downstairs and find two women
who smile at me and ask me what I think
of the Bible's predictions for the future?

Myself, I think it's safer to predict the past
and start to intone: *Sufficient unto the day
are the evils thereof.* The younger woman claims
they're sorry to have woken me, though it is midday,
– they can always call at a better time
but for now would I like to read this leaflet?

With Such Impress of Shipwrights

Nothing was rotten in the state of Denmark
– sitting on the ramparts of Elsinore,
the castle behind us invented by tradition,

and prongy enough to impound or impale a flock of clouds.
Nothing was wrong. Quite the contrary except for
time running or fading out towards the far shore

like the sheer white lines of that Swedish ferry
(which would be back for us in a couple of hours)
toiling through the channel in the year's last sun.

My head was full of striped lighthouses and traffic lights,
their tin boxes ticking. Didn't Fortinbras
go to war with your people for some patch of dirt or straw?

Nothing swithering, dithering, havering, wavering
about you, no princely antics of delay.
Your yes not ghostly but a round 'of course'.

The last time you wrote you told me Warsaw
in winter was like a big dusty thistle. But this was still, just,
    summer:
the lime tree had more leaves than the time of year

could reasonably warrant. Nothing was what you'd call wrong.
There was still time left for us to miss the boat.

The Parrot Park
(Rilke)

Under the Turkish lindens where the mown lawns end
they sway on their perches and lean half-stunned
as though a whiff of cloves and coriander
had reached them from the land they've left behind.

Alien in the green heights, they are on parade.
They keep their mad bright costumes immaculate,
stropping their beaks made of jasper and jade
and squandering the grey chaff of sunflower seeds.

Beneath their claws drab pigeons gulp down what they drop
whilst fastidiously they sift the food trough
for the one grain, the one clear taste they crave

then back to the day-job: to sulk and mock and roll their
    eyes up.
And when their tongues' dark meat has tried the rough
leg-irons, they lean back and wait for the crowd to arrive.

Bird's-eye View with Fish-eye Lens
for Simon Carnell

With nothing but culture
at his back and sides
the naturist Neptune's tall enough
for a small prospect of the waves
where the longueurs of
Kungsportsavenyn
cede to a cobbled quay.
He's weighing up the javelin
of a spiny gurnard
– its eyes on stalks, on cocktail sticks.

With time to kill, or let die,
I could visit the gallery
he's turned his back on
and check out the Strindbergs,
their black ice and cod-liver glaze
laid on with a fish-knife
or follow his gaze
down by the docks
where, in their Arctic disguise,
brinded gunboats
are dogging the hulls
of liners, but I veer
towards the palmhus exotics
for an eye to eye
with the caged cockatoo
among homesick parrots
who mope and snap at
fleas under wings

the unlikely green
of carwash rollers.

The cockatoo's amused
by the state of my plumes
and keeps screwing up
its wrinkled azure eyelid
and swivelling its neck
as though it's mounted
on an oiled sphere.
It was here in Gothenburg,
home of the Volvo,
that the engineer Wingquist
invented the ball-bearing,
'the spherical ball-bearing',
as if its prototypes
had all been pyramids
or granite bricks
– that pearl of wisdom
I got from the guidebook
I'd nothing better to do
than turn the pages of
and roll my eyeballs over.

Fish Eye

Hours of nothing biting on the lugworm bait
the twins had shown me how to catch – then suddenly
this spiny monster gurnard face appeared
banging about on the floor of the rowboat
like a fist or a heart. Way too scared
of its hackled gills and crest of spikes
to unthread the hook and heave it back
we froze, and watched its will to live abate
while a fog like a tide of opal stole
over the oily surface of the eye
extinguishing an eerie Borealis.
Were the cells desiccating in the iris?
Or divulging the inky depths to this new hemisphere
of air too thin, too dry and bright to bear?

Basilisk

The grey-green snake of the Grand Canal
heals itself behind a fleet of hulls
and white marble writes white marble on the face
of the water under the façades
in a fat oily squiggle straight from the tube.
When the tyre-clad flank of the vaporetto thuds
against the belly of the dock, we pilgrims watch
how in her sky-blue suit the blond conductress
throws an eight around the two
Arsenal-forged cast-iron bollards
and brings the boat's
stern first and then its prow
into a tame adjacency.
She might have stepped straight out of that
mural I've just been to see
where a small local female saint subdues
the scaly basilisk and leads it
still trembling with lust on a length of cord
– it must be silk – across the square and through
the parting crowd – it must be here
where the sea's edge drapes its hard green lace
on polished stones our feet perceive as waves.

Oil and Blood

Sleep on my chosen one it's only me
intent as a Madagascan sloth that moves
through the tall twilight of mahogany,
padding down the wall towards your pillowcase
and the hollows of your neck I ache for.
Lifting one knee, you shape a linen vault
that frees the scent of nard and nightflowers.
Does my dark disturb you, sweetheart, do you dream
of the rooftree burdened by a roost of bats,
your outline inscaped by their squeaky jargon?

Within a tongue's length of your ear lobe,
I could consume whole nights in this vestibule
of paradise if waiting weren't such hell
or if Van Helsing, that bony eunuch,
weren't striding upstairs with his cricket bag
full of sharpened stumps and oil of garlic,
the paraphernalia of intolerance.
Let him come. Rather than leave you be
I'd have the sun impale me and the breeze distress
my mouldy flavoured, still enamoured dust.

Right of Way

Were we expecting these toads on our doorstep?
– the smaller with a jewel stuck
to her forehead, a round white pebble,
a third eye, only blind, without a pupil,
picked up on her pilgrimage beside
the artificial lake or risking the ringroad.

It's chill and blank, that stone – perhaps a chunk
of granite ballast from the virtual quarry,
the way it seems more of an ailment
than an ornament. Her mate is clad in
eco-warrior fatigues: grey chevrons
screenprinted on a ground of dull jade.

Both have a furtive, raddled air as if
in protest at the dust fumes and the din
as the grabclaw clanks on the wagons' rim,
loading and unloading ballast. But the door open,
they make for the hallway with sagging hops
like small encrusted beanbags on the move

and seem to know, thanks all the same,
where the back door is, like it was their
house, or no house at all – their right of way
from well before we'd made such strides ahead
as building walls to live inside of, theirs before
we'd dragged our pelts and selves out of the mud.

Shaky Premises

Now timber beetles make our house their home,
bowling long galleries down the solid oak
purlins so hardwood breaks under the thumb
like a wrecked mast or an ancient sponge cake,
the whole place may hang on the shakiest premise
– hair of the hog or the horse, a coat of paint or skim –
like that alpaca jacket, years on the coat hook,
which herds of clothes moths have more or less

darned with thin air. Outside's the same:
I had such high hopes for the hollyhock
which now has one leaf left. The clematis
snails have whittled down to a dry faun stem . . .
So having been eaten out of house and home
truly our place of habitation has become
a waste of dragons – what I thought was built on rock
was draped not built, and draped on the abyss.

Beyond

I spent all morning in the café talking
to a man who'd just survived a car crash.
They'd cut him out of the wreck, his legs crushed
and still not cured – his chest a map of some
forsaken country no one could live in,
as seen from the air, which was where he was then,
or felt himself to be – looking down on his own
body picked out in a ring of light though at first at least
there was no actual light there, only a dark road.
He tried to explain to me that feeling of peace
he'd had, that even now hadn't deserted him,
but did the moment when he chose (it seems a choice
was offered him) to enter his body again,
by this time in an ambulance. He became his pain,
the pain an entire horizon of hot wire,
till the paramedics pumped him full of morphine.

I told him about your accident, Lee,
the speed you were going, not forty miles per hour,
the road, the drystone wall, the service station
forecourt opposite, the date, the cloudless sky,
how the pheasant flew up from the uncut verge
into your vizor or chest, as if I'd seen it,
as if I'd seen it from above or from beyond.
I listed your injuries and mentioned the man
who'd put your wristwatch, still ticking, inside
your ribbed black glove, wrapped you in a plaid rug
and dialled for help on his mobile while he kept
hold of your hand . . . I wanted to hear
how beyond the moment that has stained our lives

and left some part of us stranded on that verge,
beyond the fateful shiny insect torso of the bike
you'd been lifted up into what the man described.

In Arcana Fidei

You had a whole shelf of books devoted to death,
most of which I now have in my keeping.
God knows they're the last things I want
though till they'd passed to me I'd hardly guessed
how scrutable to some those last things are
– since then I've learnt, for instance, that
there's a smell like the smell of flowering lilac
which Swedenborg's angels use to dissuade
anyone approaching the spirit in transit.
It must find its feet first in the other world,
then – useless all denials – its deeds and crimes
are disinterred in their entirety
down to the coded entry in the diary,
the least bit of backbiting, the wronged maiden's
tearstained roundshouldered downcast look,
the poisoned cup, the stolen funds, the secret tryst . . .

Stockholm today is like the banished zone
where the lost have found their level – and me among them
after a sleepless night in the Blue Tower
where Strindberg died from a cancered gut, his mind gone
tortuous with alchemy and Swedenborg
– all round him poisoners: *a taste from hell,*
of brass and corpses. In the thin daylight here
– a narrow path between two blocks of night –
I'm free to stray from Drottninggaten's line
and chance on Swedenborg's own Minneskyrka
a small beached ark with Latin script that claims:
THE INTELLECT IS NOW PERMITTED
TO ENTER THE MYSTERIES OF FAITH

– a quaint undaunted other-worldly traffic sign
though the kirk's green spire, gilt crown and five-peaked star
make no inroads on a sky of solid cloud.

Coracle

Who's left to understand my dreams for me?
Della Casa in that book of manners
which took Dante to task for bad language
deemed almost all dreams worse than pointless,
especially if we have to listen to them.
But you listened to dreams with a wide-eyed,
sharp-eyed, solemn-humorous
belief in their importance. The importance,
to you, of other people's inner lives
is a source of continuing amazement to me,
and now an absent source. I can feel for
the person who left a note on your grave
(perhaps I shouldn't have read it, talking of manners):
You were the only one who believed in me.
I keep thinking you might've kept a little more
of that belief for yourself, for your own life

which could hardly have been replenished by
giving so much away. Even now when you've given
no less than everything I catch myself
wondering what on earth you'd have made of me
being ferried last night in a stone coracle
by one Eric the Red and an African pilot,
who looked like the ivory *Pequod*'s third harpooner,
to a rockpiled coast on which a village hung
somewhere I guessed must be the Western Isles . . .
With you there to hear it, it wouldn't seem so pointless
– but you've taken your skills and your odd
questing respect for the other world
to the other world, wherever that is,

however we get there – taken them with you
now when more than ever
I'm in need of them to understand.

The Belen

It all seemed natural till some strange things came
and left. Butterflies eyed with pink and ochre,
a dazzling blue beneath, sauntered through the mild air

then disappeared. The river flowed both ways at once
the way a road does, but without a barrier.
It was then the bird arrived and I stopped dead

to understand it – its feathers
were the oiled russet of crushed saffron
and sown with spots that glinted like tinfoil.

Like the ruse birds have to lure a predator
away from their nest, its brief awkward flights
seemed meant to have me follow it on

through high grass right to the ends of the earth.
I wondered was this maybe some new type
of jay or hoopoe, only bigger, or

was this the bird that crossed your path and died
beside you? A woman standing on the wooden bridge
said it's just the Belen. As a doctor

she'd seen it many times before, to her
it all seemed natural but to me that bird,
which then dipped its beak and wings and tail

behind a concealed horizon in mid-air,
diving through the line of its erasure,
was as suddenly other as being born.

Singing Lessons

Barking and yepping long before I've parked,
your dog still knows the sound, the creaks and coughs
of your Citroën I've been the sole driver of
for the now exactly four years since.
It's as though she thinks one day, just once,
as the chassis sags back on its haunch of air,
it'll be your scuffed soles on the gravel walk
and then in the hall your dark asthmatic voice.
To improve which you took singing lessons – and offence
when I mimicked your teacher's fit of despair.
What stopped me then from saying that your chesty wheeze,
wrecked with Runcorn smog, Speke's pharmaceutical haze,
was always a kind of home, not just to the dog,
and as heartening as any human song?

Sea Salt

When my attention
should have been fixed
on that girl sitting there
across the table from me
after days of thinking of nothing but
or little else,
I was distracted by a crystal
she'd shed from the salt bowl
– first of all it looked
like the kind of roof a child might put
on a painted house and then more like
a see-through pyramid,
the steps of a miniature Machu Picchu
but carved from tears and not from stone.

Salt
(Montale)

We don't know if tomorrow has green pastures
in mind for us to lie down in beside
the ever-youthful patter of fresh water
or if it means to plant us in some arid
outback ugly valley of the shadow
where dayspring's lost for good, interred beneath
a lifetime of mistakes. We'll maybe wake up
in foreign cities where the sun's a ghost,
a figment of itself and angular
starched consonants braid the tongue at its root
so all sense of who we are is lost to words,
and nothing that we know can be unravelled.
Even then, some vestige of the sea,
its plosive tide, its fretwork crests will surge
inside our syllables, bronze like the chant of bees.
However far we've stumbled from the source
a trace of the sea's voice will lodge in us
as the sunlight somehow still abides in
faded tufts that cling to bricks and kerbstones
on half-cleared slums or bomb-sites left unbuilt.
Then out of nowhere after years of silence
the words we used, our unobstructed accents,
will well up from the dark of childhood,
and once more on our lips we'll taste Greek salt.

The Ladder

They lean against the bedroom wall
– two equal parts of an extending ladder –
one going up, perhaps, the other down
or else the opposite. Their rungs a his-and-hers,

split-level, open-plan wardrobe handy
enough as it's worked out, without that being planned,
for grabbing clothes off. A split Jacob's ladder
for the two-way traffic of seraphim, itself an image

for DNA's double spiral peeled apart
or a sectioned Tantric spinal column showing
the downward voyage of the primal breath,
the upward urging of the spirit.

Worse days I wake to see the ladders both stop dead
like two lives shut before they reached this light,
at a white ceiling with no latch or hasp or hinge,
no up or down – a sealed floor, a solid lid.

By the Headstones

By the headstones are toys and flowers and birds
– budgies mainly, some owls –
with wings that mill and whirr.

The wind that sways the flowerheads
turns those wired wings in backward gyres
so their circumference is a blur.

These things should be friends or guardians
but if they fail it's no one's fault.
The owls have even sheathed their claws.

At ease in a deckchair
an old man reads the news and nods
to all who come to fill their watering-cans

to tend the small plots of their lost ones
crammed with the life of earth.

A Pair of Scales

One owl would do but two of them were sure
to stop us dead on the path which led to
a place half woody dark, half darkened wood

– each on its own branch imposing as
a stone ewer or a row of jurors
holding court in the dented evening light,

their bodies the bulk of sofa bolsters,
their heads all eyes, their eyes all seeing and their sight
pure Greek like Ionian volutes

curled in and perched on the plush columns
of themselves. The tetradrachm I was given
has essence of owl hammered into silver

with AΘE circling the head. A certificate
for the coin from a museum in Athens
cut no ice with the man from Sotheby's

when I tried to flog it to fund an air-ticket.
Drachme he explained meant to grasp with the hand
as well as the exact weight. Thus tetra: four times that.

He showed me on his scales how mine weighed more
or less, whichever. Instead he bought
an old dollar clad with an eagle grasping sticks

more than worth its weight in gold. So
unable to render into money what wasn't
money and predated Caesar, I kept the owl

nestling in its tarnished box of night
– a counterfeit, a work of art. But there on the path
the real, the rufous plumed, the twilit owls

weighed down exactly on the wood they gripped
as though in weighing up the world and us
on the tawny trays of their irises

they'd let nothing drop without its true worth
being known. It went on like a dream
– us staring at them, them staring at us –

whose sequel is the same dream, the same dim path
and need to fathom what amounts to now
(whilst the now it measures out has turned to then);

to grasp with hand or foot and sift the dusk
without spilling once an ounce of metal
from such milled and inlit, cooling eye-disks.

Cataract

A half-moon is cut into the eye-ball
and a liquid injected to dissolve
the protein of the lens, leaving the lens
capsule unscathed. Then – quite dark in there –
the silicone replacement is inserted
and opened up inside like an umbrella
or a ship in a bottle. When the patch
on your eye's removed
the world is full of brave new outlines,
even the angle-poised nuthatch
then the green woodpecker breakfasting
on a column of nuts is up closer,
vivider than ever, only it's all
unaccountably rose-tinted
with occasional flashes and upheavals
like a storm rolling over the Red Sea
observed by a rider on a camel.

Give or Take

Just how heavy the human head is
is easy indeed to underestimate.

My sister tells me it weighs-in around
12 lbs, give or take a few fluid ounces

of grey matter – she hands her pupils with backpains
a shrunken-headsized lethal *pétanque*

of pitted golden Cotswold stone
that must have once adorned a balustrade

before rolling off its stalk with a trochaic thud
and gets them to imagine walking round

with one of those balanced on their backbones
– and that's not even counting all the thoughts

which laid end to end would span the equator
and weigh as much as the world itself.

Under the Skin
for Allegra Wint

Two flutes made from a red crane's wing bone,
thousands of years old, were found – one in Denmark,

one in China; and acupuncture marks
along the liver's meridian were detected

on an Anglo-Saxon corpse – these small facts
I've been collecting for some reason show

however many thousand miles apart how
oriental, at heart, we were, or are.

'As a system,' the acupuncturist tells me,
'it's both amazingly elegant and quite barbaric

– very *Chinese* . . .' she adds with a guilty grin.
The acupoint's a miniature flute stop

about half the size of a rice grain.
Palpation discovers it under the skin

as a microchasm, a subtle dip or indent.
Since it made her fingertips blunt

– albeit in pursuit of elegance -
she finally gave up the viola

but now plays the body like an instrument
handspanning the octave of the ulna

till, unnerring, her needle finds the spot
so artesian pressure like a blown note or a wing beat

vibrates through the body's cardinal points.

Yüan Mei's Advice to his Pupils

Brave water in spate
for a pure, blue slate ink stone
(though you'll search in vain).

Ink Stain

This new jacket's wrecked with an ink stain
come through from the inside breast pocket,
black with a tell-tale edge of blue-black and maroon
thanks to a leaking gadget
patented by Laszlo Biro, the Hungarian,
and packaged by the Frenchman, Marcel Bich.
I'll have to wear it like a badge
of this scribbler's trade – alongside
the optional extra of nicotine
glazing my fingernails a tannin red –
fast-drying stuff, lightfast, semi-waterproof
(an anathema to the Chinese who judged
even bottled ink barbarian junk)
– black ink, heart's blood, mark of Cain.

But suppose that Abel was a Neanderthal
and Cain the Modern that killed him off,
less smiled on by God with his fenced settlements
and vegetable produce, but still
the one who went on to invent
biros, and write the myths of primal guilt
while the other was washed out from the gene pool
– him and his pointless stone-cobble tools,
his thick brow and pitted occipital
bulge and tender child burials, arrayed
with red deer teeth and red-ochred hide . . .
the first blood of fratricide
clotting the inkwell, crow quill or hollow reed
– sign of repentance, black bile, ox gall.

Chrome Yellow

Your three brave sunflowers are ready to drop.
Standing in a jug of stale drink
they've all about reached a steepening patch
on the curve of decay. Their dark-eyed
flameheads raddle at the tips and close,
then, lax as pulp or crape, they start to droop
on thick eyestalks. That mad Dutchman
who crammed his mouth with the chrome yellow
he used by the tubeful to paint them
made toxic lead his edible gold.
Their gold now lead, the sunflowers turn
towards the black sun of the earth.
Their time has gone. Their big leaves drape
and darken round them like a field of crows.

Will

The ghost-faced, home-based, waistcoated
solicitor all but died of kidney disease
whilst waiting for our signatures

and then on recovery – a sign of recovery? –
forbearingly sent us a host of reminders
which we kept but ignored. So much for order . . .

we'd been adult enough at the outset
though his big dog with its anger problem
had threatened to leave nothing of us remaining

larger than a nostril or a knuckle.
The man himself looked to me like Gogol
or like one of his meek, disinherited clerks

whose existence is proof of the divine smirk,
but there was no one to whom I'd have rather entrusted
what was left of my life, this paperwork.

So we willed whatever we should have thrown away
to each other in the event of some euphemism
befalling one of us. Which after three years

has yet to befall and the will, our will,
lies where it fell, always further under
the pile of papers on the occasional table,

a table not even occasionally a table
but a full-time pedestal for quires of trash.
All we had to do was pick up a pen

and, with the humblest flourish, write our names
but even that has proved beyond us,
would be an invitation to the unacceptable,

like an act of premature surrender,
like the signing of our own death warrants.

Autographs

Basil D'Oliveira and John Barbirolli,
the black man in white and the white man in black,
were the only signatures I had stuck into
my signature book. Little interested me less
than watching cricket except perhaps watching music,
but I liked the two names that were a secret rhyme
like almost acrostics. Because of his colour,
because he was a half-caste and did off-spins
and most likely with him with us we would win,
the South Africans had stopped D'Oliveira
playing, which meant the end of the whole tour.
This must have been Old Trafford, 1960-something.
Barbirolli was playing at home, away for me,
with the Manchester Hallé Orchestra.
Was Hallé French for hello or for halo?

Sir John Barbirolli hello would you sign this
(scrunched-up programme) please? He swept his coat tails
athletically round to face me as though he'd
gladly knock everyone else and everything over,
but like the wrist-roll of an elegant square-cut
he'd timed his coat-trail to a T
in that cramped backstage dressing-room
brimming with champagne and congratulations.
D'Oliveira and Barbirolli smiled elatedly
as if handing on a bat or a baton,
unaware they'd bestowed their attention
on a keck-handed, tone-deaf imposter
who wasn't collecting signatures anyway,
who just happened to be standing in the right place
and was then pushed forwards with a pen and paper.

[36]

Pasodoble

I get the key to the city cut at the kiosk's
open hatch and watch fine curlicues of steel
roll from its tongue beneath a fall of sparks

while the blind man closes up his lottery stall,
lowers his shades and mounts a motorbike.
The shiny key lies by the dull original.

Late, an engine with a Nietzschean moustache
scours the hot road, eating the red dust
as the radio's deep throat lengthens

its one note, offering its breastbone to a spike:
que tú a mí no me quieres como te quiero yo . . .
From a window comes the breathing of two runners,

neck and neck, maybe one a shade ahead, until
slowly the whole dark street begins to shudder.

The Clouds

The clouds are fiery-edged and much too low
for their own good, or ours; with a mind of their own,
they could be biding their time or ganging up.

I skulk on a humpbacked bridge whilst you placate
the host you've all but abandoned and return
in no time with your toenails painted crimson

and a pink slip showing at the golden hem.
In the square the clouds are livelier and lower still,
unleashed from a hive-shaped concrete kiln

where we'd expected a fountain or a well.
They jounce and buck in the middle air
and striking a wall or window suddenly flare

like conscience or magnesium to leave a white
powdery stain in their own round shape . . .
All so brightly sinister and picturesque

that nothing guarantees our getting out
– neither the low-cut dress your host had warned you of
nor the odd weight of these silky clouds

that glow like stars and float at the wrong height.

Suicide
(Lorca)

All the boy could bring to mind went dark
that morning, at ten o'clock.

His heart was almost bursting with
snapped wings and plastic wreaths.

What remained (without taste) in his mouth
was one word and its aftermath.

Removing his gloves he unleashed
ten slim cascades of ash.

From the balcony he saw a tower.
He felt like both that balcony and tower.

He was watched, he saw how he was watched
by the clock halted in its box.

He saw his shadow lying still and stretched
across the sofa bed's white damask.

Then rigid as a theorem, geometric,
he smashed the mirror with an axe

and the breakage let in first a trickle
and then an inundating spate of black.

Fire

(at Sant Pere de Roda)

Aside from the odd fleck of conté ochre
for the topmost clumps of olive leaves
– a brazen crown plucked from the flames – it looked like
God had sketched it all in willow charcoal
and smudged the edge with sooty fingers.
A sour stench and miles and miles of ash
– the fire had darkened everything
and only at this height run dry of fuel,
leaving jet-black tongue-marks on the buttresses
and the stone root of the monastery
before retiring. In the ruined Norman courtyard
with its deep-set, dried-up, one-eyed well,
a coin-fed wall-guide rattled through the history
of raids by Saracens, bandits, goatherds.

The last Benedictines made their getaway
bowed down with illuminated Latin
18-something, then someone stole the bell
which would have sounded out at least as far
as the bright wire of coast, just visible
from the hollow tower, beyond the burnt world where
an oily ashen stub had scribbled out
each thread of green or pulse of life
so nothing stirred, uncurled or kept account,
or breathed or browsed or crawled or delved or dwelt.
If there'd been a wind, and there wasn't, its sound
through those stumps would be the chink of anklets,
a glassy vulcan rustle saying what remains
of carbon chains is charcoal, lampblack, clinker.

No Smoke without Fire

So ingrained by now are the lessons of safe sex
even in my dreams I wear a Durex

but afterwards still crave some finecut
bright Virginia shag and the delicate

friction of rice
or liquorice.

Ceci n'est pas un pipe

Best pipe bowls are made from Corsican briar
– the bush that burns without being consumed, a tough root
with an Abrahamic, a Napoleonic strain:

the rusty iron spring, the copper vein
in the island woman's head of hair
growing back intact where it's been cut.

In Dante's Hell
(Brecht)

*The Augsberger accompanies Dante through hell. He speaks
to the hopeless cases there and tells them that on earth certain
things have changed.*

When I'd brought the pair of them the news
that up among the living nowadays
no one actually gets killed since ownership

has been abolished, the man
who wasn't, you could tell, her rightful husband
lifted his hand attached by chains to her hand,

gave her a look, then asked 'If no one can
own anything, then nothing can be stolen, right?'
I nodded, but saw that at his touch she turned

bright red. He saw it too. 'That hasn't happened
– not since that fatal moment when our lips . . .
So self-restraint's now just the same as appetite?'

And off they went, the chains that bound them tight
then seemed to weigh no more than paperclips.

Signifying Nothing

It's a long way back from the country of signs
but I made it. And now I've almost forgotten
how to say I'm old. I'm lost. I'm thirsty . . .
though I keep seeing a figure who repeats instead
one gesture where the fingers shut like a fan

or the blunt fronds of a sea-anemone
– which means, at least I think it means,
spiriting away or downright piracy.
After that, it signals nothing, nevermore, all gone
by rocking the thumb like a dorsal fin.

Chances are I'll return some day, but by then
my hands will lie by my sides as dumb as lead
weights in a sash window or loaves of bread
and once again I'll be cast on
the patience of strangers, their opacity.

The Needful

The needful thing is missing from the day
but everyone proceeds as though it's fine
– like when we waited for the nightingale
and all we heard was the army firing range;

or when the bridegroom failed to find the ring,
fumbling in the shallows of his pockets
till the priest ventured an exchange in the wording:
without this ring I wed thee anyway;

or when the iron crown of Monza
with its one nail from the true cross
was not at hand for Henry's coronation
but in a pawnshop somewhere in Milan.

A Shattered Bridge

Trouble with bridges is cows like to come
and shit on them was Jan Masaryk's riposte
to Beneš's hope the Czechlands might become
a kind of bridge between East and West.
That was before his trouble with windows
– launched of his own acccord, according
to Gottwald, from one high up the bleak
façade of Černínský palác, its thirty pillars recording
the Thirty Years' War, onto the rose, grey and black
cobblestones tourists now like to take home.
Relics bedded like molars in cold soil,
their rough cubes more picturesque than Berlin Wall.
The Ministry of Foreign Affairs' car park
now stands on the stones on which he fell –

– facing the Loreto where a single brick
dislodged from Mary's house in Nazareth
was flown by angel couriers this far north.
The vaulted niches of the courtyard wear
a collectable series of Marian apparitions:
borne by cherubs she descends like a seed-case
into chilly windswept landscapes with their place-names
on scrolls in Czech and German. The wounded skies
above a dwarfed village and a field of cows,
a disappointed bridge or shattered pier,
seem to weep pine resin or gum arabic.
Upstairs, in glass cases, lie the cobbled pearl
crucifixes, the diamond monstrance, the coral pyxes
held together by filigree braces and bridgework.

A Mole of Sorts

The digging creature has been at work again
out there – first a modest trough with a crest
of dry earth, fit for a starling or a thrush
to rest in. No big deal except to some yellow ants
doing repairs, carrying stuff on their hods.
Next day the hole was deeper,
deeper and wider, encroaching on the lawn
which yielded inch by inch each clump of turf
as though to a pendulum or scythe.

Asleep, I sat talking to an animal:
three, four foot long with silky white fur
and slim interminable fingernails
lucid as biro shafts or goose quills.
They made the plasticky click
of knitting needles as he waved them
in front of his pink snout as if to dry
the shining varnish. He was indeed,
he declared to me, a mole of sorts.

In a question of days, two weeks at most,
the lavender, the rose bush, the bay plant,
the bindweed, the lilac tree, the brambles
and the potato vine had disappeared,
leaving a long rectangular pit
like the foundations of a house
that would never be built, never be lived in.
Then I suppose that was the job done
and the digger moved on to another plot.

The Ulysses Canto
(Dante: *Inferno* XXVI)

Keep gloating, Florence, now that your great name
    has winged its way across the earth and sea
    and even hell acknowledges your fame.

There, among the thieves, I met with five
    of your choicest citizens, who made my blood
    burn in my cheeks with civic pride.

If morning dreams are dreams that tell what's true
    soon enough you'll find out what exactly
    your Tuscan neighbours have in store for you.

Soon? Why not today? Today, in my view,
    would still seem an exorbitant delay.
    Your just deserts are so long overdue.

We left – my guide helping me clamber up along
    that staircase fashioned out of mighty flagstones
    by which we'd come down earlier on -

And so resumed our lonely journey
    over the shaley rock, zigzag as a giant jigsaw
    and far easier to manage on all fours.

I felt the ache of grief. I feel it once again
    thinking back on what I saw – and need
    a kind star, at the least, to come to my aid

So I don't distrust my gift of showing forth
    the facts, and keep a sharp eye on the truth
    without getting lost in speculation.

Late summer, after sunset, when the heat abates
    and mosquitoes supplant the swarms of gnats,
    the labourer who's resting on a hillside

Sees down in the valley – where an hour before
    he'd been gathering grapes or steering the plough –
    a host of fireflies like a dust cloud or a ghost dance:

The eighth chasm was flecked like that with fires
    – tiny flames I followed with my eyes
    the moment I caught sight of the starry trough.

When bear-avenged Elisha saw the prophet's
    chariot soar, its horses reared upright
    and straining their necks towards the skies,

All he could make out was that arcing light
    rising and rising in a little cloud
    like a rocket's fiery vapour trail

– Watching those flames had the same effect
    as they sped along the ditch, and each one kept
    a sinner secret in its flickering veil.

I was on the bridge and leaning out so far
    I had to grip hard on the parapet,
    or else the least nudge would have keeled me over.

And Virgil, who saw me all eyes at this vision,
    said: 'Spirits live inside those flames
    and supply the fuel of their own combustion.'

'Dear Master,' I replied, 'now you've made clear
    the thing I'd surmised, but what I meant to ask
    was who it is that dwells inside that fire

[49]

– The one so deeply cloven down its shaft
    that it seems like the double flame that rose
    from Eteocles and his brother on the same pyre.'

His answer came: 'There in the flame is Ulysses
    wracked in tandem with Diomedes: those two
    now linked in fire as anger linked them once.

They groan within the flame for the wooden horse
    whose trapdoor opening opened up the gate
    for the whole future of the seed of Rome.

Within the flame they now lament that trick
    which left Deidemia weeping for Achilles
    and also for their theft of the Palladium.'

I begged my guide that, if the sparks could speak,
    I wouldn't have to wait for the horned flame
    to come our way but that right there and then

 It reach us. He praised my eagerness but warned me:
    'However, in this case, you must keep quiet.
    It's no big mystery what you want, so please

Let me do the talking. I have this feeling
    that, being Greeks, they'd find your mode of speech
    a shade repellent, if you'll pardon the phrase.'

So when the bidden flame had shot towards us
    and stopped where my guide had indicated,
    I heard him speak to this effect:

'You two who dwell within a single fire,
    if anything I've done has won your favour,
    if I have earned from you some small respect

When I was alive and wrote those epic lines,
   don't disappear but let the one of you
   tell where, having lost his way, he went to die.'

The taller horn of the ancient flame began
   to crimp and crumble, mumbling as it swayed
   as if a wind was tugging it from side to side

– Its tip slid back and forwards like a tongue
   in the act of speech, and then in moving
   it did speak, it spoke aloud and said:

'When I left Circe who kept me landlocked near
   that place Gaeta for a year and more
   – though it was only named by Aeneas afterwards –

No kind thought for my son nor duty towards
   my old father, nor the love I owed
   Penelope, love that might at last have gladdened her,

Could rid me of the overweening urge
   to know in full all that the world contains
   of human vice and human worth.

So I set forth on the high open sea
   with a single ship and that small company
   that remained – that hadn't died or left me.

I saw Spain pass on one side, on the other Morocco
   and saw Sardinia and the other islands
   the sea laps round. I and my men were slow

And old and tired, but still we entered
   the narrow neck of sea where Hercules
   had planted his pillars as a stop sign

[51]

For anyone meaning to pass beyond.
    Seville on our right followed Ceüta
    on our left as we ploughed on undaunted.

Brothers – I said – you who, having passed
    thousands of dangers, have now reached the West,
    to the brief span your senses may still grant you

How can you deny this experience
    of all that lies beyond the sun
    – a vast new world without a human sign?

Think what brought you out of non-existence.
    You were not made to live the life of beasts
    but to follow after virtue and knowledge.

With these few words, I honed their appetite
    to travel on to such a heightened pitch
    nothing after would have served to curb it.

We'd set our course away from dawn, veering
    always slightly south, and worked our oars
    like wings to speed us on that mad career.

Night was aswarm with stars from the other pole
    and our own familiar stars had sunk so low
    they hardly peeped above the ocean's floor.

Lit from below, five times the moon
    had filled and failed since we began
    clambering over the steep crests of the ocean

When the dim outline of the mountain
    first appeared – so huge despite the distance
    it seemed to me beyond all reckoning.

Our joy soon turned to shock when from the new land
   a storm boiled out of nowhere, shot towards us
   and slammed its head against the wooden prow.

As at someone's command, it spun us round
   three times in a gyre of foam and on the fourth
   canted the poop up in mid-air and dunked the prow

Till the sea closed over us without a trace.'